Teambuilding Questions

Concept and Development

Miguel Kagan

Designer: Alex Core
Illustrator: Erin Kant
Copyeditor: Ginny Harvey
Publications Manager: Becky Herrington

Kagan

Kagan

Kagan Publishing
981 Calle Amanecer
San Clemente, CA 92673
1 (800) 933-2667
www.KaganOnline.com

ISBN: 978-1-933445-26-7

Teambuilding Questions
TABLE OF CONTENTS

Question Card Sets

INTRODUCTION

QUICK OVERVIEW

This book offers a super simple, yet incredibly effective, way to do teambuilding. If you haven't noticed already, the book is brimming with question cards. There are 20 sets of questions and 20 question cards for each set. If my math is correct, that's 400 question cards in all! The question sets are all based on topics students love to talk about. We developed question sets on a variety of fun-to-discuss topics, including About Me, Food, Friends, Hobbies, Getting Acquainted, and more.

To play, each team receives their own set of question cards. Using RoundRobin or Spotlight (two teambuilding structures described in detail on the following pages), teammates ask and respond to the questions on the card. The stimulating questions and engaging process bring students together as a team. They get to know, like, and respect each other more. This is a tremendous benefit for students who work daily in cooperative teams. It's also a plus for the teacher who does the occasional teamwork project. And even if you don't use teamwork at all in your classroom, this teambuilding process is a wonderful way to boost class climate and make the classroom a fun place to be and learn.

If you're ready to get started, feel free to skip ahead to the Structures section. While you can use the questions in this book without using structures, you and your students will get more out of the process by using the simple teambuilding structures provided.

If you're new to teambuilding or want to explore this concept in a little more depth, read on!

WHAT IS TEAMBUILDING?

We can easily seat students in small groups and instruct them to "work together" and "be nice to each other." But that doesn't ensure successful teamwork. And it definitely doesn't guarantee students will get along well with teammates. Students come from different backgrounds, have different values, belong to different cliques, and have different ability levels. Some students simply may not want to work with others. Yuck! Others, when faced with team decisions, pull in opposite directions. With so many unique personalities, teamwork can be a challenge.

One option is to go the traditional route and forego teamwork altogether. But doing that robs students of the opportunity to work successfully in teams; to thrive in diversity; to become leaders; and to learn to work with others. Let's face it: In life and at work, personal and social skills are at least as important to our students as academic skills. But if we focused strictly on academic skills, teamwork comes out ahead again! If we forego teamwork in the classroom, we rob our students of the all the cognitive and academic benefits of teamwork. Teamwork encourages students to teach others and provides immediate help and feedback. Research shows students learn more in cooperative learning environments than in individualistic and competitive structures.

Teambuilding does require a little time and effort. But that investment of time and effort pays off—big time! With this book, we hope to minimize the effort you have to exert to reap the benefits of teambuilding.

So back to our question: What is teambuilding? Teambuilding is the process of getting individual students to feel like they are members of a team. It's the process of students getting to know and like other students on their team. It's the process of individuals coming together as a cohesive unit.

There are many different types of teambuilding activities that you can do in the classroom. We recommend that you spend a little time off academics to do the occasional teambuilding activity sheerly for fun. Teambuilding acts as a lubricant for the other interactions students have; it just makes everything run smoother.

There are a number of goals for teambuilding: We want students to discover common interests, common traits, get to know each other a little better, and feel a little more supported by teammates. Plus, we want them to learn that even though others may be different, we can understand, respect, and even celebrate those differences. Like teammates on a sports team, we want students to feel they are all on the same side and to root for each other's success. But true teamwork goes beyond just hoping for the success of your teammates. It means working together as a unit so everyone succeeds. Everyone achieves more.

WHY IS TEAMBUILDING IMPORTANT?

In the traditional classroom, teambuilding isn't essential. Students either work independently on their assignments or they actually compete against each other (as when they compete for the teacher's attention or compete for the top grades). But in the cooperative classroom, students work in teams. We have them work in teams because we know they'll learn more. And importantly, while students work in teams, students receive the added bonus of practicing ever-important social skills: learning how to be a leader, listening to each other, learning to follow directions, agreeing, helping others, negotiating understanding, solving problems together, and making group decisions. Teamwork boosts learning and creates a natural context to practice and acquire essential skills for life and the workplace.

Brain science has provided some interesting insight to teambuilding. Brain-based learning teaches us that the state of "relaxed alertness" is the optimal state for learning. Conversely, if students perceive threat in their environment, their brains "downshift" from higher-level neo-cortical functioning to more primitive limbic functioning. Fear activates the fight-or-flight mechanism and hinders students' ability to focus and learn. It is totally normal to feel anywhere between a little uneasy and downright apprehensive about strangers. It is also a well-known fact that social comparison is among the greatest stressors for humans. When people are put in situations where they are compared to others, anxiety results. Our personal worth sometimes hangs in the balance when we try to see how we stack up to others. We worry, *"How do I compare?"*

Can you think of any situations where strangers are thrust together, then evaluated on their performance? I can. It's called school. And for kids developing their own sense of identity, school can be a scary place. Think of the shy kid. The different kid. The kid who speaks a different first language. The kid who struggles in school. Those kids often perceive the classroom as a threatening place. Notice I said, "perceive." From our perspective, the classroom can be a totally safe environment, but that's not what matters; what matters is students' perceptions of the classroom. So how do we minimize the fear of strangers and anxiety-inducing social comparison?

Our answer, of course, is teambuilding. By doing regular teambuilding and giving students the opportunity to work with each other in a fun and friendly way, we lower their perceptions of threat and their stress levels. We make them feel safe. We help them perceive the classroom as a non threatening place to be and learn. Teambuilding puts students at ease and facilitates entering optimal states for learning.

WHAT'S IN THIS BOOK?

As mentioned, there are many different types of teambuilding activities. This book takes a very specific approach. It connects teambuilding questions with two terrific teambuilding structures.

Teambuilding Questions.

The book contains 400 ready-to-use question cards. The cards are organized into 20 discussion topics with 20 question cards per set. You can do a terrific, quick teambuilding activity in a few minutes with just one or two questions. With hundreds of cards, you'll have enough content here for hours and hours of teambuilding activities. While you'll probably want to mix it up and do other types of teambuilding activities during the school year, this book will provide a seemingly endless supply of questions. So if you want a quick teambuilding activity, but don't want to do any prep, pull out a question or a question card set and use these go-to staples.

The topics were selected based on things students like to discuss. The questions encourage students to share things about themselves, what they like, what they dislike, their opinions on issues, and so on. The questions promote discussion. They promote interaction. And they create fun!

Teambuilding Structures.
Structures are cooperative instructional strategies. You could use the teambuilding questions in this book as whole-class questions. But good teambuilding leverages the basic principles of cooperative learning. We use the acronym PIES to symbolize the four principles we take as core to cooperative learning. Here's how the principles relate to teambuilding:

Positive Interdependence
The task is structured so that students work together. They feel like they are on the same side.

Individual Accountability
Each student is accountable for doing something, so no student can hide.

Equal Participation
Students participate about equally.

Simultaneous Interaction
Interaction is going on in each team. If you took a snapshot of the classroom, it would show a high degree of active engagement going on within each team.

In this book, we feature two structures we encourage you to use with your students: RoundRobin and Spotlight. In RoundRobin, each teammate responds to the same question. In Spotlight, one teammate is selected to share his or her response with the team.

WHEN SHOULD I USE THESE ACTIVITIES?

- **New Teams**–Teambuilding is good to do when students first form new teams. Spending a little time on teambuilding puts students at ease with their new teammates and establishes a safe team environment for learning.

- **Weekly**–Taking a little time off academics once a week to do a little teambuilding is worth it. You can schedule the time of the week. For example, Tuesday Teambuilding at 10 o'clock for 10 minutes. Alternatively, for a little novelty, you can spring a fun teambuilding activity on the class.

- **New Students**–If you have a new student in the class, it's a good idea to do a little teambuilding. It's only natural for students to want to get to know the new teammate. It's better to provide a structured forum for getting acquainted than for students' natural inquisitiveness to interfere with what you're trying to teach.

- **Stress Reliever**–Do you or your students ever feel stressed out? How about before or after testing? Teambuilders are fun to do, and you'll see the tension literally leave their bodies as they engage in fun-to-discuss questions. And, for you too!

- **Brain-Breaks**–Break up a long block of mathematics with a teambuilder. Use the teambuilders as state changers. The teambuilders involve discussion and interaction so they work as a great state changer anytime students are doing other types of tasks such as writing, solving problems, reading, etc.

- **Energizers**– If you notice the energy level in the class is getting low, reach for a teambuilder. Students get to talk about things they like. Without fail, teambuilding questions raise the class energy level.

Question Card Tips

Each question is provided on its own question card. Individual question cards make the activity more game-like and help focus students on one question at a time. Here are a few tips for your teambuilding question cards:

- **Team Sets**—Copy a set of cards for each team. If each team has their own set of cards, you'll see much more active engagement. In a team of four, you have at least one student active at a time. Active engagement decreases in proportion to the group size. If you have one student in the class respond at a time, you only have one active participant and approximately 30 passive participants—not a good ratio.

- **Colored Paper**—Copy different sets onto different color paper to make them more colorful and easier to see at a glance that they are different sets.

- **Card Stock**—Copy the questions onto card-stock paper so the cards are more durable.

- **Laminate Cards**—Laminate the cards for extra durability.

- **Storing Cards**—Wrap a rubber band around each set of cards to keep the set together. That makes it really easy to give each team their own set of cards. Or keep sets together with an alligator clip or inside an envelope.

ROUNDROBIN

One student on the team draws one question card, then each teammate takes a turn responding.

▶ **GETTING READY:**

- Each team receives a set of question cards.

- The team stacks the set of questions face-down in the center of their team table.

Teammate Draws Question Card

1 A teammate is randomly selected to draw the first question card. The teammate draws the card and reads it aloud to the team. The teammate gives the team 5–10 seconds to think about how they'll respond.

Teammates Respond

2 Starting with the student who read the card, each teammate takes a turn sharing his or her response to the question.

Continue

3 Once every teammate has responded, the card is retired and the next teammate clockwise draws the next card. Starting with the student who read the card, each teammate takes a turn sharing his or her response to the question.

Teambuilding Structure
SPOTLIGHT

Which teammate will be under the spotlight? In Spotlight, one teammate is randomly selected to stand and respond to the question card in front of the team.

▶ **GETTING READY:**

• Each team receives a set of question cards.

• The team stacks the set of questions facedown in the center of their team table.

Think Time

2 The teacher gives everyone 5–10 seconds to think about how they'll respond if selected.

Teammate Draws Question Card

1 The teacher randomly selects one teammate on each team to draw the first question card and read it aloud to the team.

Teambuilding Questions
Kagan Publishing • (800) 933-2667 • www.KaganOnline.com

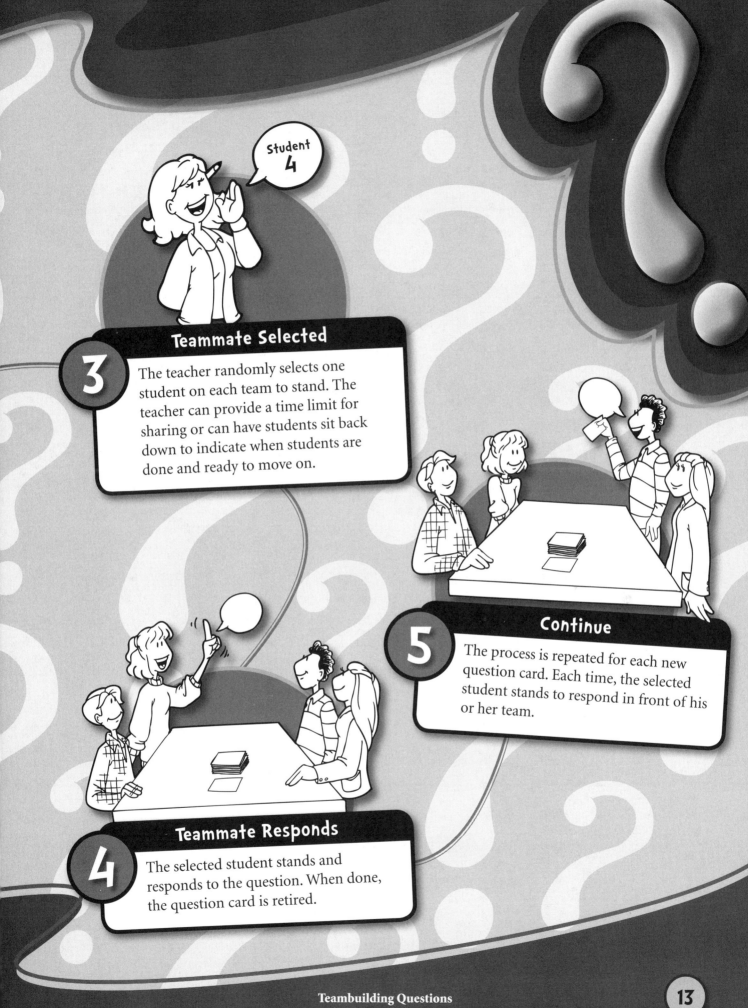

Student 4

3 Teammate Selected

The teacher randomly selects one student on each team to stand. The teacher can provide a time limit for sharing or can have students sit back down to indicate when students are done and ready to move on.

4 Teammate Responds

The selected student stands and responds to the question. When done, the question card is retired.

5 Continue

The process is repeated for each new question card. Each time, the selected student stands to respond in front of his or her team.

card set
#**1**

ABOUT ME

ABOUT ME
Question Cards

① ABOUT ME

What are three things that you are thankful for?

Teambuilding Questions • © Kagan Publishing

② ABOUT ME

What is your favorite thing to do and why?

Teambuilding Questions • © Kagan Publishing

③ ABOUT ME

What is your nickname and how did you get it? If you don't have one, what nickname would you like and why?

Teambuilding Questions • © Kagan Publishing

④ ABOUT ME

How would you describe your best friend?

Teambuilding Questions • © Kagan Publishing

Teambuilding Questions
Kagan Publishing • (800) 933-2667 • www.KaganOnline.com

ABOUT ME
Question Cards

⑤ ABOUT ME

When are you happiest and why?

Teambuilding Questions • © Kagan Publishing

⑥ ABOUT ME

What makes you really angry? Why does it make you so angry?

Teambuilding Questions • © Kagan Publishing

⑦ ABOUT ME

Who is your hero and how are you alike or different?

Teambuilding Questions • © Kagan Publishing

⑧ ABOUT ME

Complete the following sentence: One thing not many people know about me is…

Teambuilding Questions • © Kagan Publishing

 # ABOUT ME
Question Cards

⑨ ABOUT ME

If you could have anything you wanted for your birthday, what would it be and why?

Teambuilding Questions • © Kagan Publishing

⑩ ABOUT ME

What activities do you really enjoy with your family?

Teambuilding Questions • © Kagan Publishing

⑪ ABOUT ME

What is one of the scariest things that has ever happened to you and why was it scary?

Teambuilding Questions • © Kagan Publishing

⑫ ABOUT ME

What is the bravest act you've ever performed? Describe what you did.

Teambuilding Questions • © Kagan Publishing

Teambuilding Questions
Kagan Publishing • (800) 933-2667 • www.KaganOnline.com

ABOUT ME
Question Cards

13 **ABOUT ME**

If you could win a prize, what prize would it be? Describe what you'd do with it.

Teambuilding Questions • © Kagan Publishing

14 **ABOUT ME**

What is one of your favorite movies, books, or TV shows (pick one)? Describe what makes it your favorite.

Teambuilding Questions • © Kagan Publishing

15 **ABOUT ME**

What would you do with one million dollars?

Teambuilding Questions • © Kagan Publishing

16 **ABOUT ME**

What are three things you want to do before you die?

Teambuilding Questions • © Kagan Publishing

ABOUT ME
Question Cards

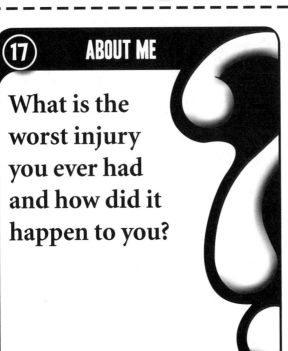

17 ABOUT ME

What is the worst injury you ever had and how did it happen to you?

Teambuilding Questions • © Kagan Publishing

18 ABOUT ME

If you could only save three things from your burning room, what would you grab?

Teambuilding Questions • © Kagan Publishing

19 ABOUT ME

Where is one place you've never been and would love to go? What makes you choose this place?

Teambuilding Questions • © Kagan Publishing

20 ABOUT ME

What is a nice thing you have done for someone else that nobody knows about? What were the circumstances?

Teambuilding Questions • © Kagan Publishing

ABOUT ME
Journal Writing Question

If you could win a prize, what prize would it be? Describe what you'd do with it.

_____

_____

_____

_____

_____

_____

_____

_____

_____

_____

_____

_____

_____

_____

_____

_____

_____

ABOUT ME
Journal Writing Question

What is one of your favorite movies, books, or TV shows (pick one)? Describe what makes it your favorite.

_____

_____

_____

_____

_____

_____

_____

_____

_____

_____

_____

_____

_____

_____

_____

_____

_____

card set
#**2**

AMUSEMENT
PARKS

AMUSEMENT PARKS
Question Cards

① AMUSEMENT PARKS

What is the scariest ride you have ever ridden? Describe it.

Teambuilding Questions • © Kagan Publishing

② AMUSEMENT PARKS

If you could go to any amusement park for your birthday, which one would you choose? Why?

Teambuilding Questions • © Kagan Publishing

③ AMUSEMENT PARKS

On a scale of 1 to 10, how much do you enjoy amusement parks? Describe.

Teambuilding Questions • © Kagan Publishing

④ AMUSEMENT PARKS

If you could design a roller coaster, what would it be like?

Teambuilding Questions • © Kagan Publishing

Teambuilding Questions
Kagan Publishing • (800) 933-2667 • www.KaganOnline.com

AMUSEMENT PARKS
Question Cards

---

5 **AMUSEMENT PARKS**

Do you prefer roller coasters, water rides, thrill rides, or family rides? Why is it your favorite type of ride?

Teambuilding Questions • © Kagan Publishing

---

6 **AMUSEMENT PARKS**

What is your favorite food to eat at an amusement park? Describe why you like it?

Teambuilding Questions • © Kagan Publishing

---

7 **AMUSEMENT PARKS**

What is the coolest show you've ever seen? Describe it.

Teambuilding Questions • © Kagan Publishing

---

8 **AMUSEMENT PARKS**

On a scale of 1 to 5, how much of a thrill seeker are you? Five is the most aggressive thrill seeker. Describe where you are on this scale and why.

Teambuilding Questions • © Kagan Publishing

AMUSEMENT PARKS
Question Cards

⑨ AMUSEMENT PARKS

If you could invite just one friend to go to an amusement park with you, who would you choose and why?

Teambuilding Questions • © Kagan Publishing

⑩ AMUSEMENT PARKS

How long would you wait in line to ride your favorite ride? How do you pass the time when you're waiting in the long line?

Teambuilding Questions • © Kagan Publishing

⑪ AMUSEMENT PARKS

Name an amusement park you've never been to before but would love to go to. Why does it look so fun?

Teambuilding Questions • © Kagan Publishing

⑫ AMUSEMENT PARKS

Do you think amusement park rides are safe? Why or why not?

Teambuilding Questions • © Kagan Publishing

Teambuilding Questions
Kagan Publishing • (800) 933-2667 • www.KaganOnline.com

AMUSEMENT PARKS
Question Cards

13 **AMUSEMENT PARKS**

Who in your family is the bravest roller coaster rider? Describe.

Teambuilding Questions • © Kagan Publishing

14 **AMUSEMENT PARKS**

If you were in charge of creating a show for a theme park based on an animated movie, what animated movie would it be? Describe the show.

Teambuilding Questions • © Kagan Publishing

15 **AMUSEMENT PARKS**

Have you ever done a full loop? Describe what it felt like. If not, describe what you think it would feel like.

Teambuilding Questions • © Kagan Publishing

16 **AMUSEMENT PARKS**

When you ride roller coasters, do you keep your hands in the air, or do you grip the safety bar tightly? Or, are you some-where in the middle? Describe.

Teambuilding Questions • © Kagan Publishing

AMUSEMENT PARKS
Question Cards

---

17 **AMUSEMENT PARKS**

Which amusement parks have you been to? Which one was your favorite so far and why?

Teambuilding Questions • © Kagan Publishing

---

18 **AMUSEMENT PARKS**

When was the last time you went to an amusement park? What was the occasion?

Teambuilding Questions • © Kagan Publishing

---

19 **AMUSEMENT PARKS**

Have you ever been terrified to ride a ride? Describe it. How did you feel after you rode it? Would you ride it again?

Teambuilding Questions • © Kagan Publishing

---

20 **AMUSEMENT PARKS**

If you could create your own amusement park, what would you name it? What would be its theme? Describe it.

Teambuilding Questions • © Kagan Publishing

Teambuilding Questions
Kagan Publishing • (800) 933-2667 • www.KaganOnline.com

AMUSEMENT PARKS
Journal Writing Question

Do you prefer roller coasters, water rides, thrill rides, or family rides? Why is it your favorite type of ride?

_____

_____

_____

_____

_____

_____

_____

_____

_____

_____

_____

_____

_____

_____

_____

_____

AMUSEMENT PARKS
Journal Writing Question

If you were in charge of creating a show for a theme park based on an animated movie, what animated movie would it be? Describe the show.

card set
#**3**

BOOKS

BOOKS
Question Cards

1 BOOKS

What is the best book you have ever read? Describe it.

2 BOOKS

Do you believe reading a book is much better for your brain than watching TV? Defend your position.

3 BOOKS

Who is your favorite author? What makes him or her your favorite?

4 BOOKS

Do you prefer stories that are realistic or stories that are not believable? Explain your preference.

Teambuilding Questions
Kagan Publishing • (800) 933-2667 • www.KaganOnline.com

BOOKS
Question Cards

---

5 **BOOKS**

If you could jump into any book and become part of the story, which would you choose and why?

---

6 **BOOKS**

If you could be any character from any book, who would you be and why?

---

7 **BOOKS**

Have you ever read a book that was wildly funny? If yes, which one and what was so funny? If not, how could you find one? Would you read it?

---

8 **BOOKS**

What is one book that was so exciting or interesting, you just couldn't put it down? Why was it such a page-turner?

BOOKS
Question Cards

⑨ BOOKS

Do you prefer stories that are set in the past, present, or future? Explain.

Teambuilding Questions • © Kagan Publishing

⑩ BOOKS

Complete the following sentence: Books are…

Teambuilding Questions • © Kagan Publishing

⑪ BOOKS

If you were going to write a book, what would you write about?

Teambuilding Questions • © Kagan Publishing

⑫ BOOKS

If you were going to write an autobiography, on which events in your life would you focus?

Teambuilding Questions • © Kagan Publishing

Teambuilding Questions
Kagan Publishing • (800) 933-2667 • www.KaganOnline.com

BOOKS
Question Cards

13 | **BOOKS**

What is one thing you've learned from reading?

Teambuilding Questions • © Kagan Publishing

14 | **BOOKS**

Do you have a special time or place that you read? Describe how it enhances your reading experience.

Teambuilding Questions • © Kagan Publishing

15 | **BOOKS**

Pick a character from a book you've read and describe how he or she changed over the course of the story.

Teambuilding Questions • © Kagan Publishing

16 | **BOOKS**

Which book would you like the author to write a sequel? What would happen in the sequel?

Teambuilding Questions • © Kagan Publishing

BOOKS
Question Cards

17 BOOKS

Have you read a book and then seen a movie based on the book? How is a book like and unlike a movie?

18 BOOKS

What is your favorite genre of books? (Adventure, humor, romance, horror, fantasy, science fiction, or historical.) Explain why you think this genre appeals to you.

19 BOOKS

What is one book that you would change the ending to? How would you change it?

20 BOOKS

Pretend you are a literary critic. Give a quick review of the last book you read.

BOOKS
Journal Writing Question

If you were going to write an autobiography, on which events in your life would you focus?

BOOKS
Journal Writing Question

Pick a character from a book you've read and describe how he or she changed over the course of the story.

_____

_____

_____

_____

_____

_____

_____

_____

_____

_____

_____

_____

_____

_____

_____

_____

Teambuilding Questions
Kagan Publishing • (800) 933-2667 • www.KaganOnline.com

CELEBRITIES

CELEBRITIES
Question Cards

CELEBRITIES
1 If you could hang out with a celebrity for an entire day, who would you choose? What would you do?

Teambuilding Questions • © Kagan Publishing

CELEBRITIES
2 Would you rather be a celebrity for being an actor, musician, or athlete? Explain.

Teambuilding Questions • © Kagan Publishing

CELEBRITIES
3 Do celebrities deserve the millions of dollars they make? Explain why you feel this way.

Teambuilding Questions • © Kagan Publishing

CELEBRITIES
4 Do celebrities have any special responsibilities? What are they?

Teambuilding Questions • © Kagan Publishing

Teambuilding Questions
Kagan Publishing • (800) 933-2667 • www.KaganOnline.com

CELEBRITIES
Question Cards

CELEBRITIES

5

Do you think being a celebrity would be an easy life? Why or why not?

Teambuilding Questions • © Kagan Publishing

CELEBRITIES

6

Why do you think that people who actually are more talented than some celebrities never become famous?

Teambuilding Questions • © Kagan Publishing

CELEBRITIES

7

If you were a celebrity, how would you use your wealth and fame toward a good cause?

Teambuilding Questions • © Kagan Publishing

CELEBRITIES

8

If you ran into a celebrity in the grocery store, how would you act?

Teambuilding Questions • © Kagan Publishing

CELEBRITIES
Question Cards

CELEBRITIES

9

Do you think most celebrities become famous because they love what they do or because they love the fame? What could be another reason people become celebrities?

Teambuilding Questions • © Kagan Publishing

CELEBRITIES

10

Would you rather be rich or famous? Explain.

Teambuilding Questions • © Kagan Publishing

CELEBRITIES

11

Which celebrity do you think might become even more popular? What makes you feel this way?

Teambuilding Questions • © Kagan Publishing

CELEBRITIES

12

If you were a celebrity and read something hurtful and completely untrue about yourself in a gossip magazine, what would you do?

Teambuilding Questions • © Kagan Publishing

CELEBRITIES
Question Cards

13 CELEBRITIES

Celebrities often make a lot of money endorsing a product. Pick a celebrity and state what product(s) he or she could endorse because of their fame.

Teambuilding Questions • © Kagan Publishing

14 CELEBRITIES

Do you think it's fair that critics ridicule celebrities for the way they dress just because they're in the spotlight?

Teambuilding Questions • © Kagan Publishing

15 CELEBRITIES

If you could win an award for being a celebrity, which award would you most want to win and why?

Teambuilding Questions • © Kagan Publishing

16 CELEBRITIES

Do you believe that celebrities have earned the right to be rude to others? Explain your position.

Teambuilding Questions • © Kagan Publishing

CELEBRITIES
Question Cards

CELEBRITIES (17)

If you could trade places with a famous athlete for the rest of your life, who would you choose and why?

Teambuilding Questions • © Kagan Publishing

CELEBRITIES (18)

If you were asked to be on a reality TV show, but it would mean you'd have to drop out of school and move to another city, would you do it?

Teambuilding Questions • © Kagan Publishing

CELEBRITIES (19)

What is your biggest celebrity moment?

Teambuilding Questions • © Kagan Publishing

CELEBRITIES (20)

Who is one celebrity that has given a bad name to other stars in their industry (for example, movies, music, sports, etc.)? What should be the consequences?

Teambuilding Questions • © Kagan Publishing

Teambuilding Questions
Kagan Publishing • (800) 933-2667 • www.KaganOnline.com

CELEBRITIES
Journal Writing Question

If you could hang out with a celebrity for an entire day, who would you choose? What would you do?

_____

_____

_____

_____

_____

_____

_____

_____

_____

_____

_____

_____

_____

_____

_____

_____

_____

_____

CELEBRITIES
Journal Writing Question

If you were a celebrity, how would you use your wealth and fame toward a good cause?

Teambuilding Questions
Kagan Publishing • (800) 933-2667 • www.KaganOnline.com

FAMILY

FAMILY
Question Cards

① FAMILY

What is one thing you really enjoy doing with your family? Describe it.

② FAMILY

Do you have family holiday traditions? Describe one.

③ FAMILY

What is the best vacation you've been on with your family? Describe it.

④ FAMILY

Do you have any brothers or sisters? If so, describe them. If not, do you like being an only child?

Teambuilding Questions
Kagan Publishing • (800) 933-2667 • www.KaganOnline.com

FAMILY
Question Cards

5 FAMILY

Are you the oldest, youngest, or middle child? Do you think this has anything to do with your personality? Explain.

Teambuilding Questions • © Kagan Publishing

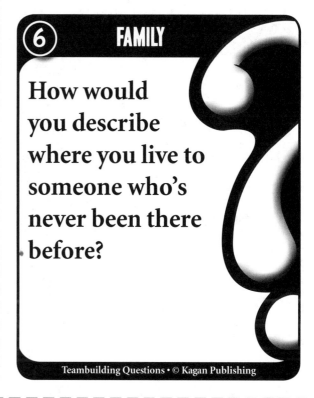

6 FAMILY

How would you describe where you live to someone who's never been there before?

Teambuilding Questions • © Kagan Publishing

7 FAMILY

Does your family enjoy playing any games together? Describe the one that's particularly fun.

Teambuilding Questions • © Kagan Publishing

8 FAMILY

How long have you lived in your current family home? How did you come to live there?

Teambuilding Questions • © Kagan Publishing

FAMILY
Question Cards

9 FAMILY

What chores or responsibilities do you have in your family? Explain.

Teambuilding Questions • © Kagan Publishing

10 FAMILY

Are your grandparents still living? Do you see them often? What is your relationship with them? Describe it.

Teambuilding Questions • © Kagan Publishing

11 FAMILY

What do you know about your last name? How would you go about tracing your family name?

Teambuilding Questions • © Kagan Publishing

12 FAMILY

Do you have a famous person in your family tree? If so, describe him or her. If not, what famous person would you like to have in your family? Why?

Teambuilding Questions • © Kagan Publishing

Teambuilding Questions
Kagan Publishing • (800) 933-2667 • www.KaganOnline.com

FAMILY
Question Cards

13 — FAMILY

What is your best family memory? Give details.

Teambuilding Questions • © Kagan Publishing

14 — FAMILY

Pick two people from your family, and describe how they are alike and how they are different.

Teambuilding Questions • © Kagan Publishing

15 — FAMILY

What was the last fun thing you did with your family? Describe it.

Teambuilding Questions • © Kagan Publishing

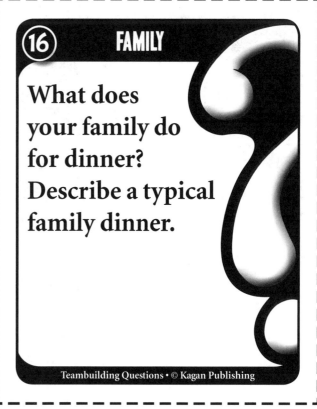

16 — FAMILY

What does your family do for dinner? Describe a typical family dinner.

Teambuilding Questions • © Kagan Publishing

FAMILY
Question Cards

17   **FAMILY**

What have you learned from your parents?

Teambuilding Questions • © Kagan Publishing

18   **FAMILY**

Complete the following sentence. My family…

Teambuilding Questions • © Kagan Publishing

19   **FAMILY**

Do you have a big family or small family? What makes your family unique?

Teambuilding Questions • © Kagan Publishing

20   **FAMILY**

Would you change anything about your family if you could? What would it be?

Teambuilding Questions • © Kagan Publishing

Teambuilding Questions
Kagan Publishing • (800) 933-2667 • www.KaganOnline.com

FAMILY
Journal Writing Question

What is the best vacation you've been on with your family? Describe it.

_____

_____

_____

_____

_____

_____

_____

_____

_____

_____

_____

_____

_____

_____

_____

_____

_____

FAMILY
Journal Writing Question

How would you describe where you live to someone who's never been there before?

_____

_____

_____

_____

_____

_____

_____

_____

_____

_____

_____

_____

_____

_____

_____

_____

_____

_____

Teambuilding Questions
Kagan Publishing • (800) 933-2667 • www.KaganOnline.com

card set
#6

FOOD

FOOD
Question Cards

1 — **FOOD**

What is your favorite dessert? Describe it in detail.

Teambuilding Questions • © Kagan Publishing

2 — **FOOD**

What do you consider junk food? When do you think it is okay to eat junk food?

Teambuilding Questions • © Kagan Publishing

3 — **FOOD**

Describe the perfect breakfast.

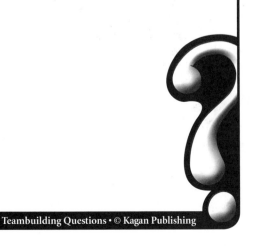

Teambuilding Questions • © Kagan Publishing

4 — **FOOD**

What is one food you can't stand and why?

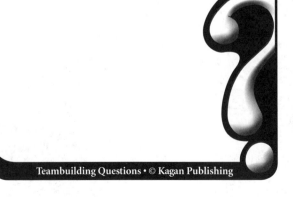

Teambuilding Questions • © Kagan Publishing

Teambuilding Questions
Kagan Publishing • (800) 933-2667 • www.KaganOnline.com

FOOD
Question Cards

5 **FOOD**

What is your favorite meal of the day? Why?

Teambuilding Questions • © Kagan Publishing

6 **FOOD**

What is your favorite snack?

Teambuilding Questions • © Kagan Publishing

7 **FOOD**

Does anyone in your family have a special dish that they prepare? Who? What is the dish?

Teambuilding Questions • © Kagan Publishing

8 **FOOD**

Would you rather eat out at a restaurant or eat at home? Describe.

Teambuilding Questions • © Kagan Publishing

FOOD
Question Cards

9   **FOOD**

What is the difference between a healthy meal and an unhealthy meal?

Teambuilding Questions • © Kagan Publishing

10   **FOOD**

What is one food you simply could not live without? Why?

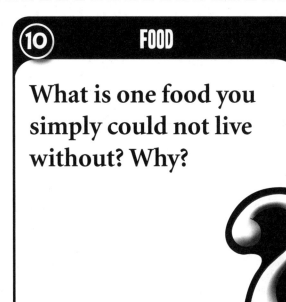

Teambuilding Questions • © Kagan Publishing

11   **FOOD**

Do you prefer salty, sweet, or spicy foods? Describe.

Teambuilding Questions • © Kagan Publishing

12   **FOOD**

Do you eat more fruits or more vegetables? Describe.

Teambuilding Questions • © Kagan Publishing

FOOD
Question Cards

---

13 · FOOD

What is your favorite fast food restaurant? What do you order when you go there?

Teambuilding Questions • © Kagan Publishing

---

14 · FOOD

Complete the following sentence. Food is…

Teambuilding Questions • © Kagan Publishing

---

15 · FOOD

Would you consider yourself a picky eater? Explain.

Teambuilding Questions • © Kagan Publishing

---

16 · FOOD

Do you have any rules about food in your household? If so, describe them. If not, what rules might be good for your family?

Teambuilding Questions • © Kagan Publishing

FOOD
Question Cards

17   **FOOD**

What kind of cooking or food preparation tasks do you have? What could you do to help more?

18   **FOOD**

Who cooks the meals in your family? How do you rate the taste and variety? What would you change, if anything?

19   **FOOD**

What would you do if you were eating dinner at a friend's house and you didn't like the meal they were serving?

20   **FOOD**

What would you order at a Mexican restaurant? Describe it.

FOOD
Journal Writing Question

What do you consider junk food? When do you think it is okay to eat junk food?

FOOD
Journal Writing Question

What would you do if you were eating dinner at a friend's house and you didn't like the meal they were serving?

_____

_____

_____

_____

_____

_____

_____

_____

_____

_____

_____

_____

_____

_____

_____

_____

_____

card set #7

FRIENDS

FRIENDS
Question Cards

1 **FRIENDS**

Who is your best friend and why? How did you meet your best friend?

Teambuilding Questions • © Kagan Publishing

2 **FRIENDS**

Would you rather have one or two close friends or a lot of friendly acquaintances? Explain why you feel this way.

Teambuilding Questions • © Kagan Publishing

3 **FRIENDS**

Describe one of your best friends to someone who has never met him or her.

Teambuilding Questions • © Kagan Publishing

4 **FRIENDS**

What is your favorite thing to do with friends?

Teambuilding Questions • © Kagan Publishing

Teambuilding Questions
Kagan Publishing • (800) 933-2667 • www.KaganOnline.com

FRIENDS
Question Cards

⑤ FRIENDS

Has one of your best friends ever moved away? How did it make you feel? Are you still friends? If not, how do you think you would feel if it happened?

Teambuilding Questions • © Kagan Publishing

⑥ FRIENDS

If you could invite one friend to go on vacation with you, which friend would you invite and where would you go?

Teambuilding Questions • © Kagan Publishing

⑦ FRIENDS

How is your best friend like you? How is that friend unlike you?

Teambuilding Questions • © Kagan Publishing

⑧ FRIENDS

Are you ever jealous of your friends? Or, has a friend ever been jealous of you? Describe how you feel.

Teambuilding Questions • © Kagan Publishing

FRIENDS
Question Cards

---

⑨ FRIENDS

Do you ever fight with your friends? If so, how do you make up? If not, how do you avoid fighting?

Teambuilding Questions • © Kagan Publishing

---

⑩ FRIENDS

When did you and your best friend decide to call each other best friends? Describe your common interest or characteristic.

Teambuilding Questions • © Kagan Publishing

---

⑪ FRIENDS

What is one thing you have in common with three of your friends?

Teambuilding Questions • © Kagan Publishing

---

⑫ FRIENDS

Pick two friends and describe how they are alike and how they are different.

Teambuilding Questions • © Kagan Publishing

Teambuilding Questions
Kagan Publishing • (800) 933-2667 • www.KaganOnline.com

FRIENDS
Question Cards

---

13 **FRIENDS**

Have you and your friend ever been in trouble together? What did you do to get into trouble? What happened to the friendship because of it?

---

14 **FRIENDS**

What one characteristic do you have that makes you a good friend? Give an example.

---

15 **FRIENDS**

Have you ever stopped being friends with somebody? What happened that caused you to end your friendship?

---

16 **FRIENDS**

If you could trade places with one of your friends for a full day, which friend would you choose and why?

 **FRIENDS**
Question Cards

17 FRIENDS

What qualities do you look for in a friend?

Teambuilding Questions • © Kagan Publishing

18 FRIENDS

Do you dress like your friends? How so or how not?

Teambuilding Questions • © Kagan Publishing

19 FRIENDS

What quality would you like to improve on to be a better friend? Explain.

Teambuilding Questions • © Kagan Publishing

20 FRIENDS

If you were going to plan a perfect day for you and your friend, what would you do?

Teambuilding Questions • © Kagan Publishing

Teambuilding Questions
Kagan Publishing • (800) 933-2667 • www.KaganOnline.com

FRIENDS
Journal Writing Question

Would you rather have one or two close friends or a lot of friendly acquaintances? Explain why you feel this way.

_____

_____

_____

_____

_____

_____

_____

_____

_____

_____

_____

_____

_____

_____

_____

_____

_____

FRIENDS
Journal Writing Question

What one characteristic do you have that makes you a good friend? Give an example.

_____

_____

_____

_____

_____

_____

_____

_____

_____

_____

_____

_____

_____

_____

_____

_____

_____

_____

_____

_____

Teambuilding Questions
Kagan Publishing • (800) 933-2667 • www.KaganOnline.com

card set
#8

GETTING ACQUAINTED

GETTING ACQUAINTED
Question Cards

GETTING ACQUAINTED

1

How would your mother describe you?

Teambuilding Questions • © Kagan Publishing

GETTING ACQUAINTED

2

What makes you mad? Explain how it happens.

Teambuilding Questions • © Kagan Publishing

GETTING ACQUAINTED

3

What brings a smile to your face? Describe.

Teambuilding Questions • © Kagan Publishing

GETTING ACQUAINTED

4

Who is your inspiration? Why?

Teambuilding Questions • © Kagan Publishing

GETTING ACQUAINTED
Question Cards

GETTING ACQUAINTED

⑤ What are you most proud of? Explain.

Teambuilding Questions • © Kagan Publishing

GETTING ACQUAINTED

⑥ What are your strengths? How do you think you achieved these strengths?

Teambuilding Questions • © Kagan Publishing

GETTING ACQUAINTED

⑦ What are your weaknesses? How do you think you can improve?

Teambuilding Questions • © Kagan Publishing

GETTING ACQUAINTED

⑧ What do you cherish most? Why?

Teambuilding Questions • © Kagan Publishing

GETTING ACQUAINTED
Question Cards

GETTING ACQUAINTED

9

If you could have any job, what would you choose? Why?

Teambuilding Questions • © Kagan Publishing

GETTING ACQUAINTED

10

What can you tell me about yourself?

Teambuilding Questions • © Kagan Publishing

GETTING ACQUAINTED

11

What event in your personal history had the biggest impact on you? When was it?

Teambuilding Questions • © Kagan Publishing

GETTING ACQUAINTED

12

How would you describe your typical day?

Teambuilding Questions • © Kagan Publishing

Teambuilding Questions
Kagan Publishing • (800) 933-2667 • www.KaganOnline.com

GETTING ACQUAINTED
Question Cards

GETTING ACQUAINTED

13

What is the biggest obstacle you have had to overcome? Explain.

Teambuilding Questions • © Kagan Publishing

GETTING ACQUAINTED

14

What do you believe in? Who has influenced you in these beliefs?

Teambuilding Questions • © Kagan Publishing

GETTING ACQUAINTED

15

How would you describe your personality to someone you've never met?

Teambuilding Questions • © Kagan Publishing

GETTING ACQUAINTED

16

What is the one thing not many people know about you?

Teambuilding Questions • © Kagan Publishing

GETTING ACQUAINTED
Question Cards

GETTING ACQUAINTED

17

Would you rather be rich or famous? Explain.

Teambuilding Questions • © Kagan Publishing

GETTING ACQUAINTED

18

If you could go anywhere in the world for one week, where would you go? What would you do?

Teambuilding Questions • © Kagan Publishing

GETTING ACQUAINTED

19

If you could be a famous person in history, who would it be and why?

Teambuilding Questions • © Kagan Publishing

GETTING ACQUAINTED

20

What is your goal for your future?

Teambuilding Questions • © Kagan Publishing

Teambuilding Questions
Kagan Publishing • (800) 933-2667 • www.KaganOnline.com

GETTING ACQUAINTED
Journal Writing Question

What event in your personal history had the biggest impact on you? When was it?

_____

_____

_____

_____

_____

_____

_____

_____

_____

_____

_____

_____

_____

_____

_____

_____

_____

GETTING ACQUAINTED
Journal Writing Question

If you could go anywhere in the world for one week, where would you go? What would you do?

_____

_____

_____

_____

_____

_____

_____

_____

_____

_____

_____

_____

_____

_____

_____

_____

_____

Teambuilding Questions
Kagan Publishing • (800) 933-2667 • www.KaganOnline.com

HOBBIES

HOBBIES
Question Cards

1 HOBBIES

What is your favorite hobby? Describe it?

Teambuilding Questions • © Kagan Publishing

2 HOBBIES

What is one hobby you'd like to try that you've never tried? Why?

Teambuilding Questions • © Kagan Publishing

3 HOBBIES

How is a hobby like a sport? How is it different?

Teambuilding Questions • © Kagan Publishing

4 HOBBIES

Do you have friends who share your hobby? Explain.

Teambuilding Questions • © Kagan Publishing

HOBBIES
Question Cards

5 **HOBBIES**

How did you get interested in your favorite hobby? How did you learn it?

Teambuilding Questions • © Kagan Publishing

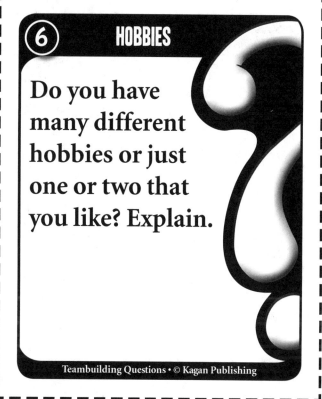

6 **HOBBIES**

Do you have many different hobbies or just one or two that you like? Explain.

Teambuilding Questions • © Kagan Publishing

7 **HOBBIES**

What hobby sounds more fun to you: bird-watching, gardening, or keeping an aquarium? Why?

Teambuilding Questions • © Kagan Publishing

8 **HOBBIES**

Do you prefer board games, card games, or computer games? Explain.

Teambuilding Questions • © Kagan Publishing

HOBBIES
Question Cards

⑨ HOBBIES

Do you collect anything? If yes, what? If no, what is something collectible that would interest you?

Teambuilding Questions • © Kagan Publishing

⑩ HOBBIES

What is your best creation ever? Describe it.

Teambuilding Questions • © Kagan Publishing

⑪ HOBBIES

If you were given a canvas, paints, and a brush, what would you paint? Describe the painting.

Teambuilding Questions • © Kagan Publishing

⑫ HOBBIES

Would you consider your favorite hobby safe or dangerous? Why?

Teambuilding Questions • © Kagan Publishing

HOBBIES
Question Cards

13 HOBBIES

How often do you do your hobby? For how long? Explain.

Teambuilding Questions • © Kagan Publishing

14 HOBBIES

Do you like to read for fun? If yes, describe what you like to read. If no, how could you become more interested in reading?

Teambuilding Questions • © Kagan Publishing

15 HOBBIES

Do you sub-scribe to any magazines? If yes, describe the magazine(s). If no, what maga-zine would you like to subscribe to and why?

Teambuilding Questions • © Kagan Publishing

16 HOBBIES

What is your favorite thing to ride with wheels? When and where do you ride? Why do you like it?

Teambuilding Questions • © Kagan Publishing

HOBBIES
Question Cards

17 HOBBIES

Do you prefer indoor activities or outdoor activities? Why?

Teambuilding Questions • © Kagan Publishing

18 HOBBIES

If you could build a room just for your hobby, what would the room look like?

Teambuilding Questions • © Kagan Publishing

19 HOBBIES

What hobby do you think might interest you when you get older?

Teambuilding Questions • © Kagan Publishing

20 HOBBIES

What are the positive and negative aspects of your favorite hobby?

Teambuilding Questions • © Kagan Publishing

Teambuilding Questions
Kagan Publishing • (800) 933-2667 • www.KaganOnline.com

HOBBIES
Journal Writing Question

If you were given a canvas, paints, and a brush, what would you paint? Describe the painting.

HOBBIES
Journal Writing Question

What is your favorite thing to ride with wheels? When and where do you ride? Why do you like it?

_____

_____

_____

_____

_____

_____

_____

_____

_____

_____

_____

_____

_____

_____

_____

_____

_____

_____

Teambuilding Questions
Kagan Publishing • (800) 933-2667 • www.KaganOnline.com

card set
#10

HOLIDAYS

HOLIDAYS
Question Cards

1 **HOLIDAYS**

What is your number-one favorite holiday? How do you celebrate it?

Teambuilding Questions • © Kagan Publishing

2 **HOLIDAYS**

What is one family holiday tradition that you treasure and why?

Teambuilding Questions • © Kagan Publishing

3 **HOLIDAYS**

Many holidays are celebrated to recognize a famous person. Which famous person do you think is deserving of a holiday and why?

Teambuilding Questions • © Kagan Publishing

4 **HOLIDAYS**

How much does your family celebrate and decorate for the holidays?

Teambuilding Questions • © Kagan Publishing

Teambuilding Questions
Kagan Publishing • (800) 933-2667 • www.KaganOnline.com

HOLIDAYS
Question Cards

⑤   **HOLIDAYS**

What is your favorite holiday song? Sing what you can.

Teambuilding Questions • © Kagan Publishing

⑥   **HOLIDAYS**

What is your favorite holiday dish or treat? Describe it in full detail.

Teambuilding Questions • © Kagan Publishing

⑦   **HOLIDAYS**

If today was Thanksgiving, what would you say you are most thankful for and why?

Teambuilding Questions • © Kagan Publishing

⑧   **HOLIDAYS**

What is your favorite holiday memory? Describe it.

Teambuilding Questions • © Kagan Publishing

HOLIDAYS
Question Cards

⑨ HOLIDAYS

What is something great you've done to show your love on Father's Day or Mother's Day?

Teambuilding Questions • © Kagan Publishing

⑩ HOLIDAYS

Complete the following sentence: I love holidays because…

Teambuilding Questions • © Kagan Publishing

⑪ HOLIDAYS

Why do you think different cultures celebrate different holidays? Can you name an international holiday?

Teambuilding Questions • © Kagan Publishing

⑫ HOLIDAYS

Do you think there is one holiday that everyone in the world should celebrate? If yes, describe it. If not, why not?

Teambuilding Questions • © Kagan Publishing

Teambuilding Questions
Kagan Publishing • (800) 933-2667 • www.KaganOnline.com

HOLIDAYS
Question Cards

13 | **HOLIDAYS**

Do you prefer to travel or stay at home for the holiday? Where do you usually go if you travel?

Teambuilding Questions • © Kagan Publishing

14 | **HOLIDAYS**

What is the funniest April Fools' Day practical joke you've ever played or are aware of?

Teambuilding Questions • © Kagan Publishing

15 | **HOLIDAYS**

Pick one holiday and describe the meaning of it to you personally.

Teambuilding Questions • © Kagan Publishing

16 | **HOLIDAYS**

When you think of Halloween, what comes to mind? Tell as many things as you can think of.

Teambuilding Questions • © Kagan Publishing

HOLIDAYS
Question Cards

---

17 | **HOLIDAYS**

Do you think schools and businesses should be closed for everyone on all holidays? Explain your position.

Teambuilding Questions • © Kagan Publishing

---

18 | **HOLIDAYS**

What are the differences between religious and public holidays?

Teambuilding Questions • © Kagan Publishing

---

19 | **HOLIDAYS**

What's the difference between a national holiday and an unofficial holiday? Name one of each.

Teambuilding Questions • © Kagan Publishing

---

20 | **HOLIDAYS**

What was the last holiday you celebrated, and how did you celebrate it?

Teambuilding Questions • © Kagan Publishing

Teambuilding Questions
Kagan Publishing • (800) 933-2667 • www.KaganOnline.com

What is your favorite holiday dish or treat? Describe it in full detail.

HOLIDAYS
Journal Writing Question

Do you think there is one holiday that everyone in the world should celebrate? If yes, describe it. If not, why not?

_____

_____

_____

_____

_____

_____

_____

_____

_____

_____

_____

_____

_____

_____

_____

_____

_____

Teambuilding Questions
Kagan Publishing • (800) 933-2667 • www.KaganOnline.com

card set
#**11**

MOVIES

MOVIES
Question Cards

Teambuilding Questions
Kagan Publishing • (800) 933-2667 • www.KaganOnline.com

MOVIES
Question Cards

5 **MOVIES**

Do you prefer animated movies or movies with live actors? Explain why.

Teambuilding Questions • © Kagan Publishing

6 **MOVIES**

Do you agree or disagree that sequels are never as good as the original movie? Give some examples to support your position.

Teambuilding Questions • © Kagan Publishing

7 **MOVIES**

What is the last movie you saw? How would you rate it and why?

Teambuilding Questions • © Kagan Publishing

8 **MOVIES**

Do you prefer to see movies at home or in the movie theaters? Why?

Teambuilding Questions • © Kagan Publishing

MOVIES
Question Cards

---

9 **MOVIES**

What movie do you really want to see? Why?

Teambuilding Questions • © Kagan Publishing

---

10 **MOVIES**

Why do you think it takes so many people to make a movie?

Teambuilding Questions • © Kagan Publishing

---

11 **MOVIES**

Would you rather be an actor, a director, a stuntman, or a screenplay writer? Why?

Teambuilding Questions • © Kagan Publishing

---

12 **MOVIES**

What is the funniest movie you've ever seen? Describe it.

Teambuilding Questions • © Kagan Publishing

MOVIES
Question Cards

13 | **MOVIES**

Do you like sad movies? Why or why not?

Teambuilding Questions • © Kagan Publishing

14 | **MOVIES**

Pick one movie character and describe him or her as best as you can.

Teambuilding Questions • © Kagan Publishing

15 | **MOVIES**

Who is your favorite movie villain and why?

Teambuilding Questions • © Kagan Publishing

16 | **MOVIES**

What is your favorite song from a movie? Why do you like it so much?

Teambuilding Questions • © Kagan Publishing

MOVIES
Question Cards

17 MOVIES

Which movie do you think has the best special effects and why?

Teambuilding Questions • © Kagan Publishing

18 MOVIES

Complete the following sentence. Movies are…

Teambuilding Questions • © Kagan Publishing

19 MOVIES

What movie influenced you the most and why?

Teambuilding Questions • © Kagan Publishing

20 MOVIES

If you could make a movie about an event in your life, which event would you choose? Describe it.

Teambuilding Questions • © Kagan Publishing

MOVIES
Journal Writing Question

Who is your favorite actor? Which movie or movies did you like him or her best in and why?

_____

_____

_____

_____

_____

_____

_____

_____

_____

_____

_____

_____

_____

_____

_____

_____

_____

MOVIES
Journal Writing Question

What is the funniest movie you've ever seen? Describe it.

_____

_____

_____

_____

_____

_____

_____

_____

_____

_____

_____

_____

_____

_____

_____

_____

_____

Teambuilding Questions
Kagan Publishing • (800) 933-2667 • www.KaganOnline.com

MUSIC

MUSIC
Question Cards

MUSIC ①

Name your favorite band. Why do you like the band?

Teambuilding Questions • © Kagan Publishing

MUSIC ②

Do you think today's musicians are more talented, or original, than musicians of the past? Why or why not?

Teambuilding Questions • © Kagan Publishing

MUSIC ③

What is the best concert you've ever seen? What made it better than others you attended?

Teambuilding Questions • © Kagan Publishing

MUSIC ④

Do you play any musical instruments? If yes, which one(s)? If not, which instrument(s) would you like to play? Why?

Teambuilding Questions • © Kagan Publishing

Teambuilding Questions
Kagan Publishing • (800) 933-2667 • www.KaganOnline.com

MUSIC
Question Cards

MUSIC

5

Do you think music in school should be required? Or, should it be an elective only? Why?

Teambuilding Questions • © Kagan Publishing

MUSIC

6

What is your favorite genre of music? What genre of music do you least like?

Teambuilding Questions • © Kagan Publishing

MUSIC

7

What is your favorite song? Why do you like it so much?

Teambuilding Questions • © Kagan Publishing

MUSIC

8

When and where do you listen to music? How does it make you feel?

Teambuilding Questions • © Kagan Publishing

MUSIC
Question Cards

MUSIC

9

Who has had the most influence on your musical preferences? How?

Teambuilding Questions • © Kagan Publishing

MUSIC

10

If you were in a band, would you rather sing or play an instrument? Which instrument? Describe your preference.

Teambuilding Questions • © Kagan Publishing

MUSIC

11

If you formed a band, what would you call it? How would you decide?

Teambuilding Questions • © Kagan Publishing

MUSIC

12

Would you want to be a rock-star? Why or why not?

Teambuilding Questions • © Kagan Publishing

MUSIC
Question Cards

MUSIC

13

What is your favorite music video? Describe it.

Teambuilding Questions • © Kagan Publishing

MUSIC

14

If you could have any band play at your next birthday party, which band would it be? Why that band?

Teambuilding Questions • © Kagan Publishing

MUSIC

15

How have your musical preferences changed over time?

Teambuilding Questions • © Kagan Publishing

MUSIC

16

How can different kinds of music put you in different moods? Describe.

Teambuilding Questions • © Kagan Publishing

MUSIC
Question Cards

MUSIC **17**

How has technology affected the way we make and listen to music?

Teambuilding Questions • © Kagan Publishing

MUSIC **18**

Should downloading music over the Internet be illegal? Why or why not?

Teambuilding Questions • © Kagan Publishing

MUSIC **19**

Do you pay more attention to the lyrics of music or just the sound and rhythm of music?

Teambuilding Questions • © Kagan Publishing

MUSIC **20**

Who is the most talented musician that you personally know? Describe him or her?

Teambuilding Questions • © Kagan Publishing

MUSIC
Journal Writing Question

What is your favorite music video? Describe it.

_____

_____

_____

_____

_____

_____

_____

_____

_____

_____

_____

_____

_____

_____

_____

_____

_____

MUSIC
Journal Writing Question

Should downloading music over the Internet be illegal? Why or why not?

_____

_____

_____

_____

_____

_____

_____

_____

_____

_____

_____

_____

_____

_____

_____

_____

_____

Teambuilding Questions
Kagan Publishing • (800) 933-2667 • www.KaganOnline.com

RATE YOURSELF

RATE YOURSELF
Question Cards

---

1 **RATE YOURSELF**

How honest are you? Explain your rating.

Teambuilding Questions • © Kagan Publishing

---

2 **RATE YOURSELF**

How funny are you? Explain your rating.

Teambuilding Questions • © Kagan Publishing

---

3 **RATE YOURSELF**

How smart are you? Explain your rating.

Teambuilding Questions • © Kagan Publishing

---

4 **RATE YOURSELF**

How happy are you? Explain your rating.

Teambuilding Questions • © Kagan Publishing

Teambuilding Questions
Kagan Publishing • (800) 933-2667 • www.KaganOnline.com

RATE YOURSELF
Question Cards

⑤ RATE YOURSELF

How friendly are you? Explain your rating.

Teambuilding Questions • © Kagan Publishing

⑥ RATE YOURSELF

How athletic are you? Explain your rating.

Teambuilding Questions • © Kagan Publishing

⑦ RATE YOURSELF

How energetic are you? Explain your rating.

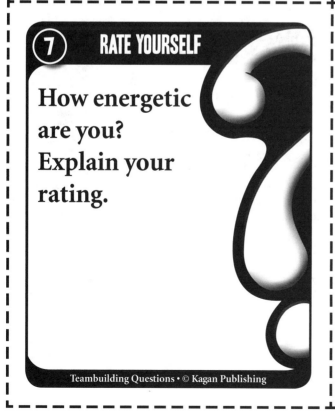

Teambuilding Questions • © Kagan Publishing

⑧ RATE YOURSELF

How responsible are you? Explain your rating.

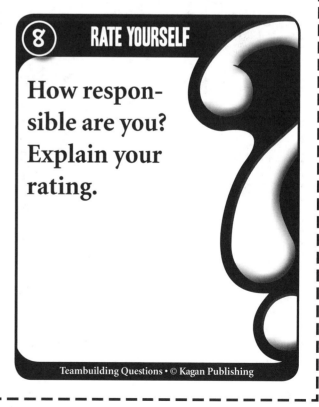

Teambuilding Questions • © Kagan Publishing

RATE YOURSELF
Question Cards

9 RATE YOURSELF

How self-centered are you? Explain your rating.

Teambuilding Questions • © Kagan Publishing

10 RATE YOURSELF

How generous are you? Explain your rating.

Teambuilding Questions • © Kagan Publishing

11 RATE YOURSELF

How thankful are you? Explain your rating.

Teambuilding Questions • © Kagan Publishing

12 RATE YOURSELF

How kind are you? Explain your rating.

Teambuilding Questions • © Kagan Publishing

RATE YOURSELF
Question Cards

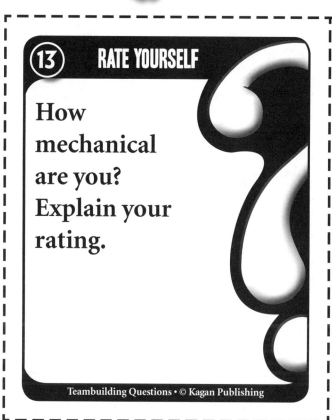

13 **RATE YOURSELF**

How mechanical are you? Explain your rating.

Teambuilding Questions • © Kagan Publishing

14 **RATE YOURSELF**

How social are you? Explain your rating.

Teambuilding Questions • © Kagan Publishing

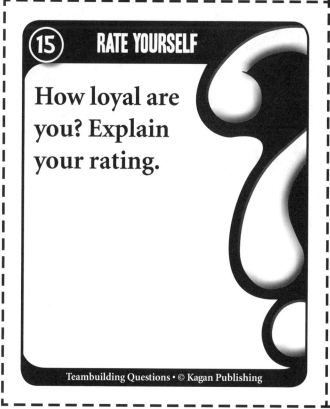

15 **RATE YOURSELF**

How loyal are you? Explain your rating.

Teambuilding Questions • © Kagan Publishing

16 **RATE YOURSELF**

How adventurous are you? Explain your rating.

Teambuilding Questions • © Kagan Publishing

RATE YOURSELF
Question Cards

17 RATE YOURSELF

How respectful are you? Explain your rating.

Teambuilding Questions • © Kagan Publishing

18 RATE YOURSELF

How hard-working are you? Explain your rating.

Teambuilding Questions • © Kagan Publishing

19 RATE YOURSELF

How creative are you? Explain your rating.

Teambuilding Questions • © Kagan Publishing

20 RATE YOURSELF

How confident are you? Explain your rating.

Teambuilding Questions • © Kagan Publishing

Teambuilding Questions
Kagan Publishing • (800) 933-2667 • www.KaganOnline.com

RATE YOURSELF
Journal Writing Question

How thankful are you? Explain your rating.

_____

_____

_____

_____

_____

_____

_____

_____

_____

_____

_____

_____

_____

_____

_____

_____

_____

_____

RATE YOURSELF
Journal Writing Question

How creative are you?
Explain your rating.

_____

_____

_____

_____

_____

_____

_____

_____

_____

_____

_____

_____

_____

_____

_____

_____

_____

Teambuilding Questions
Kagan Publishing • (800) 933-2667 • www.KaganOnline.com

card set
#14

SCHOOL

SCHOOL
Question Cards

1 **SCHOOL**

Do you think uniforms should be required or a school dress code should be enforced? Explain.

Teambuilding Questions • © Kagan Publishing

2 **SCHOOL**

Should you be allowed to play on a school team if you have bad grades? How do you think that would make other teammates feel?

Teambuilding Questions • © Kagan Publishing

3 **SCHOOL**

Should high school students be allowed to go off campus during lunch? Why or why not?

Teambuilding Questions • © Kagan Publishing

4 **SCHOOL**

Should fast food or junk food be served in the school cafeteria? Why or why not?

Teambuilding Questions • © Kagan Publishing

Teambuilding Questions
Kagan Publishing • (800) 933-2667 • www.KaganOnline.com

SCHOOL
Question Cards

5 | **SCHOOL**

Do you agree or disagree that physical exercise should be mandatory for every student in school? Explain the benefits.

Teambuilding Questions • © Kagan Publishing

6 | **SCHOOL**

Complete the following sentence. School is...

Teambuilding Questions • © Kagan Publishing

7 | **SCHOOL**

Who is the best teacher you've ever had and why?

Teambuilding Questions • © Kagan Publishing

8 | **SCHOOL**

What is your favorite subject? Why do you like it so much?

Teambuilding Questions • © Kagan Publishing

SCHOOL
Question Cards

9 SCHOOL

Art and music are just as important as math and science. Do you agree or disagree?

10 SCHOOL

Which subject is your least favorite? Why?

11 SCHOOL

How do you get to school? Describe your typical commute.

12 SCHOOL

What do you like best about your school? Explain.

Teambuilding Questions
Kagan Publishing • (800) 933-2667 • www.KaganOnline.com

SCHOOL
Question Cards

13 | **SCHOOL**

If you could change one thing about school, what would you change? Why?

Teambuilding Questions • © Kagan Publishing

14 | **SCHOOL**

Have you ever received any kind of award in school? If yes, what for? If no, which award would you most want?

Teambuilding Questions • © Kagan Publishing

15 | **SCHOOL**

Who takes the most interest in your education? Describe.

Teambuilding Questions • © Kagan Publishing

16 | **SCHOOL**

Do you feel a lot of peer pressure in your school? Describe.

Teambuilding Questions • © Kagan Publishing

SCHOOL
Question Cards

17 | **SCHOOL**

Do you have any friends who are homeschooled? What do you think are the advantages to being home-schooled? Are there disadvantages?

Teambuilding Questions • © Kagan Publishing

18 | **SCHOOL**

What are the benefits of year-round school? Would you want to be on the year-round schedule? Why or why not?

Teambuilding Questions • © Kagan Publishing

19 | **SCHOOL**

Have you ever had a tutor? What are the benefits of learning with a tutor? If not, how could a tutor help you with your most difficult subject?

Teambuilding Questions • © Kagan Publishing

20 | **SCHOOL**

Have you been called on to answer a question in class you were not prepared for? If no, how would you feel? What would you do?

Teambuilding Questions • © Kagan Publishing

Teambuilding Questions
Kagan Publishing • (800) 933-2667 • www.KaganOnline.com

SCHOOL
Journal Writing Question

What is your favorite subject?
Why do you like it so much?

_____

_____

_____

_____

_____

_____

_____

_____

_____

_____

_____

_____

_____

_____

_____

_____

_____

_____

_____

SCHOOL
Journal Writing Question

If you could change one thing about school, what would you change? Why?

_____

_____

_____

_____

_____

_____

_____

_____

_____

_____

_____

_____

_____

_____

_____

_____

_____

_____

Teambuilding Questions
Kagan Publishing • (800) 933-2667 • www.KaganOnline.com

SHOULD KIDS....

SHOULD KIDS...
Question Cards

1 SHOULD KIDS...

Should kids be allowed to buy whatever they want with their own money? Why? How do you earn your own money?

Teambuilding Questions • © Kagan Publishing

2 SHOULD KIDS...

Should kids under 18 be allowed to get tattoos? Why or Why not?

Teambuilding Questions • © Kagan Publishing

3 SHOULD KIDS...

Should kids be allowed to play violent video games? What kind of an influence do you think they have?

Teambuilding Questions • © Kagan Publishing

4 SHOULD KIDS...

Should kids be allowed to watch R-rated movies? Have you watched one? Why do you think movies are rated?

Teambuilding Questions • © Kagan Publishing

SHOULD KIDS...
Question Cards

---

(5) SHOULD KIDS...

Should kids be allowed to listen to music with explicit lyrics? Why do you think these lyrics could be damaging?

---

(6) SHOULD KIDS...

Should kids be limited to how much TV they are allowed to watch? What negative results could come from viewing too much TV?

---

(7) SHOULD KIDS...

Should kids be allowed to skip school if they don't feel like going? How can you justify them being allowed to do that?

---

(8) SHOULD KIDS...

Should toy guns and other violent toys for kids be banned? Explain your stance.

SHOULD KIDS...
Question Cards

⑨ SHOULD KIDS...

Should playing a sport be mandatory for all kids? Do the benefits support this kind of rule? Explain.

Teambuilding Questions • © Kagan Publishing

⑩ SHOULD KIDS...

Should playing an instrument be mandatory for kids? How would you feel if you were required to learn an instrument?

Teambuilding Questions • © Kagan Publishing

⑪ SHOULD KIDS...

Should boys and girls have separate classes? If yes, should they be taught separate subjects? If no, why not?

Teambuilding Questions • © Kagan Publishing

⑫ SHOULD KIDS...

Should parents be allowed to discipline their children by spanking or hitting them? What are better ways? Explain your position.

Teambuilding Questions • © Kagan Publishing

Teambuilding Questions
Kagan Publishing • (800) 933-2667 • www.KaganOnline.com

SHOULD KIDS...
Question Cards

13 **SHOULD KIDS...**

Should kids be allowed to work? Would you want to work? Why or why not?

Teambuilding Questions • © Kagan Publishing

14 **SHOULD KIDS...**

Should prayer be allowed in school? Defend your position.

Teambuilding Questions • © Kagan Publishing

15 **SHOULD KIDS...**

Should kids be kicked out of school for bullying? Why or why not? How can you prevent bullying?

Teambuilding Questions • © Kagan Publishing

16 **SHOULD KIDS...**

Should all the smartest kids be put in the same class? How does that affect kids who don't make the grades but might be just as smart?

Teambuilding Questions • © Kagan Publishing

SHOULD KIDS...
Question Cards

17 **SHOULD KIDS...**

Should children under the age of 13 be allowed to stay home alone? Why? What would you do to be safe and act responsibly if you were home alone?

Teambuilding Questions • © Kagan Publishing

18 **SHOULD KIDS...**

Should kids be required to wear a helmet while riding a bike or skateboard? Why or why not?

Teambuilding Questions • © Kagan Publishing

19 **SHOULD KIDS...**

Should kids be allowed to wear whatever they want to school? Why or why not? Why do you think there is a dress code?

Teambuilding Questions • © Kagan Publishing

20 **SHOULD KIDS...**

Should parents be punished for the mistakes their kids make? Explain. What do you think is an alternative to parents being punished?

Teambuilding Questions • © Kagan Publishing

Teambuilding Questions
Kagan Publishing • (800) 933-2667 • www.KaganOnline.com

SHOULD KIDS...
Journal Writing Question

Should playing an instrument be mandatory for kids? How would you feel if you were required to learn an instrument?

_____

_____

_____

_____

_____

_____

_____

_____

_____

_____

_____

_____

_____

_____

_____

_____

_____

_____

SHOULD KIDS...
Journal Writing Question

Should parents be allowed to discipline their children by spanking or hitting them? What are better ways? Explain your position.

Teambuilding Questions
Kagan Publishing • (800) 933-2667 • www.KaganOnline.com

TEAMS

TEAMS
Question Cards

TEAMS

1 Complete the following sentence. Our team is…

Teambuilding Questions • © Kagan Publishing

TEAMS

2 Do you have any special roles and responsibilities in your team? Why were you assigned your role?

Teambuilding Questions • © Kagan Publishing

TEAMS

3 What is your best experience being in this team? Describe.

Teambuilding Questions • © Kagan Publishing

TEAMS

4 Create a special team handshake and show your teammates.

Teambuilding Questions • © Kagan Publishing

Teambuilding Questions
Kagan Publishing • (800) 933-2667 • www.KaganOnline.com

TEAMS
Question Cards

TEAMS

5

Pick one teammate and say what you appreciate most about that teammate.

Teambuilding Questions • © Kagan Publishing

TEAMS

6

How could the team run more effectively? Explain.

Teambuilding Questions • © Kagan Publishing

TEAMS

7

Do you believe that there is strength in diversity? Explain. Do you have a personal experience with it?

Teambuilding Questions • © Kagan Publishing

TEAMS

8

How do teammates help each other?

Teambuilding Questions • © Kagan Publishing

TEAMS
Question Cards

TEAMS

9

Do you feel like your teammates are on your side? Why or why not?

Teambuilding Questions • © Kagan Publishing

TEAMS

10

Does everyone on the team participate about equally? Explain.

Teambuilding Questions • © Kagan Publishing

TEAMS

11

What kinds of problems can you solve in a team that you cannot solve on your own? Describe.

Teambuilding Questions • © Kagan Publishing

TEAMS

12

What is the difference between coaching and giving the answer? Explain how to coach.

Teambuilding Questions • © Kagan Publishing

Teambuilding Questions
Kagan Publishing • (800) 933-2667 • www.KaganOnline.com

TEAMS
Question Cards

TEAMS

13

Team stands for Together Everyone Achieves More, TEAM. Do you believe this is true? Explain.

Teambuilding Questions • © Kagan Publishing

TEAMS

14

What could you do if conflict exists within your team? Explain.

Teambuilding Questions • © Kagan Publishing

TEAMS

15

What are some examples of working in teams in the real world?

Teambuilding Questions • © Kagan Publishing

TEAMS

16

What does it mean to be a team player? Are you a team player? How can you tell?

Teambuilding Questions • © Kagan Publishing

TEAMS
Question Cards

17 | **TEAMS**

What is your team's greatest accomplishment? Describe it.

Teambuilding Questions • © Kagan Publishing

18 | **TEAMS**

How is a team in the classroom similar to a sports team? How is it different?

Teambuilding Questions • © Kagan Publishing

19 | **TEAMS**

What could you do if different teammates came up with different answers? Do you think there would be conflict?

Teambuilding Questions • © Kagan Publishing

20 | **TEAMS**

Why is good communication important for a team? How well does your team communicate?

Teambuilding Questions • © Kagan Publishing

Teambuilding Questions
Kagan Publishing • (800) 933-2667 • www.KaganOnline.com

TEAMS
Journal Writing Question

What kinds of problems can you solve in a team that you cannot solve on your own? Describe.

_____

_____

_____

_____

_____

_____

_____

_____

_____

_____

_____

_____

_____

_____

TEAMS
Journal Writing Question

What are some examples of working in teams in the real world?

_____

_____

_____

_____

_____

_____

_____

_____

_____

_____

_____

_____

_____

_____

_____

_____

_____

Teambuilding Questions
Kagan Publishing • (800) 933-2667 • www.KaganOnline.com

TELL ME ABOUT...

TELL ME ABOUT...
Question Cards

① TELL ME ABOUT...

Tell me about your family.

Teambuilding Questions • © Kagan Publishing

② TELL ME ABOUT...

Tell me about your room.

Teambuilding Questions • © Kagan Publishing

③ TELL ME ABOUT...

Tell me about your goals for the future.

Teambuilding Questions • © Kagan Publishing

④ TELL ME ABOUT...

Tell me about your fears.

Teambuilding Questions • © Kagan Publishing

Teambuilding Questions
Kagan Publishing • (800) 933-2667 • www.KaganOnline.com

TELL ME ABOUT...
Question Cards

---

5 TELL ME ABOUT...

Tell me about school.

Teambuilding Questions • © Kagan Publishing

---

6 TELL ME ABOUT...

Tell me about your typical day.

Teambuilding Questions • © Kagan Publishing

---

7 TELL ME ABOUT...

Tell me about something funny you've seen or done.

Teambuilding Questions • © Kagan Publishing

---

8 TELL ME ABOUT...

Tell me about something that bothered or confused you that you had a hard time dealing with.

Teambuilding Questions • © Kagan Publishing

TELL ME ABOUT...

Question Cards

⑨ TELL ME ABOUT...

Tell me about something I don't know about you.

Teambuilding Questions • © Kagan Publishing

⑩ TELL ME ABOUT...

Tell me about a place that is special to you.

Teambuilding Questions • © Kagan Publishing

⑪ TELL ME ABOUT...

Tell me about something that you treasure.

Teambuilding Questions • © Kagan Publishing

⑫ TELL ME ABOUT...

Tell me about someone you love.

Teambuilding Questions • © Kagan Publishing

Teambuilding Questions
Kagan Publishing • (800) 933-2667 • www.KaganOnline.com

TELL ME ABOUT...
Question Cards

13 TELL ME ABOUT...

Tell me about something you can't stand.

Teambuilding Questions • © Kagan Publishing

14 TELL ME ABOUT...

Tell me about something from your past that had a big impact on you.

Teambuilding Questions • © Kagan Publishing

15 TELL ME ABOUT...

Tell me about something you're really proud of.

Teambuilding Questions • © Kagan Publishing

16 TELL ME ABOUT...

Tell me about something hard to believe that really happened.

Teambuilding Questions • © Kagan Publishing

TELL ME ABOUT...
Question Cards

17   TELL ME ABOUT...

Tell me about something interesting that you've read recently.

Teambuilding Questions • © Kagan Publishing

18   TELL ME ABOUT...

Tell me about something you know a lot about.

Teambuilding Questions • © Kagan Publishing

19   TELL ME ABOUT...

Tell me about what's been on your mind a lot.

Teambuilding Questions • © Kagan Publishing

20   TELL ME ABOUT...

Tell me about your dreams.

Teambuilding Questions • © Kagan Publishing

Teambuilding Questions
Kagan Publishing • (800) 933-2667 • www.KaganOnline.com

TELL ME ABOUT...
Journal Writing Question

Tell me about something hard to believe that really happened.

_____

_____

_____

_____

_____

_____

_____

_____

_____

_____

_____

_____

_____

_____

_____

_____

_____

_____

TELL ME ABOUT...
Journal Writing Question

Tell me about something you know a lot about.

VIDEO
GAMES

VIDEO GAMES
Question Cards

---

1 VIDEO GAMES

What is your favorite video game and why?

Teambuilding Questions • © Kagan Publishing

---

2 VIDEO GAMES

How are video games different today than they were in the past?

Teambuilding Questions • © Kagan Publishing

---

3 VIDEO GAMES

Do you think playing violent video games make people more violent in real life? Explain your stance.

Teambuilding Questions • © Kagan Publishing

---

4 VIDEO GAMES

What is a video game addict? Would you consider yourself a video game addict? Why or why not?

Teambuilding Questions • © Kagan Publishing

Teambuilding Questions
Kagan Publishing • (800) 933-2667 • www.KaganOnline.com

VIDEO GAMES
Question Cards

5 | VIDEO GAMES

How does playing video games affect you emotionally?

Teambuilding Questions • © Kagan Publishing

6 | VIDEO GAMES

If you could design your own video game, how would you play it?

Teambuilding Questions • © Kagan Publishing

7 | VIDEO GAMES

What is the best video game console and why?

Teambuilding Questions • © Kagan Publishing

8 | VIDEO GAMES

What are some positive things kids learn by playing video games? What have you learned?

Teambuilding Questions • © Kagan Publishing

VIDEO GAMES
Question Cards

⑨ VIDEO GAMES

What are some possible negative consequences of playing video games too often?

Teambuilding Questions • © Kagan Publishing

⑩ VIDEO GAMES

How are video games like board games? How are they different?

Teambuilding Questions • © Kagan Publishing

⑪ VIDEO GAMES

If you could jump into any video game and become part of the game, which one would it be and why?

Teambuilding Questions • © Kagan Publishing

⑫ VIDEO GAMES

Every video game should be rated for age appropriateness and kids shouldn't be allowed to play games beyond their age rating. Do you agree or disagree?

Teambuilding Questions • © Kagan Publishing

VIDEO GAMES
Question Cards

---

13 | **VIDEO GAMES**

What video games and gear do you have?

Teambuilding Questions • © Kagan Publishing

---

14 | **VIDEO GAMES**

If you were given the choice of playing video games or going outside to play, which would you choose? Describe.

Teambuilding Questions • © Kagan Publishing

---

15 | **VIDEO GAMES**

Have you played any video games that have frightened you or made you uncomfortable? Explain.

Teambuilding Questions • © Kagan Publishing

---

16 | **VIDEO GAMES**

Do you think boys and girls have different attitudes toward and playing habits with video games? Explain.

Teambuilding Questions • © Kagan Publishing

VIDEO GAMES
Question Cards

(17) VIDEO GAMES

Are you better at games that require strategic thinking or at games that require good eye-hand coordination? Explain.

Teambuilding Questions • © Kagan Publishing

(18) VIDEO GAMES

What are your parents' attitudes toward video games? How do they feel about your playing habits?

Teambuilding Questions • © Kagan Publishing

(19) VIDEO GAMES

What is your favorite sports-related video game? Why do you like it so much?

Teambuilding Questions • © Kagan Publishing

(20) VIDEO GAMES

If you were the president of the video game rating committee, what kind of rating system would you propose?

Teambuilding Questions • © Kagan Publishing

Teambuilding Questions
Kagan Publishing • (800) 933-2667 • www.KaganOnline.com

VIDEO GAMES
Journal Writing Question

If you could design your own video game, how would you play it?

_____
_____
_____
_____
_____
_____
_____
_____
_____
_____
_____
_____
_____
_____
_____
_____
_____
_____
_____
_____
_____

VIDEO GAMES
Journal Writing Question

What are some positive things kids learn by playing video games? What have you learned?

Teambuilding Questions
Kagan Publishing • (800) 933-2667 • www.KaganOnline.com

WEEKEND

WEEKEND
Question Cards

1 **WEEKEND**

What would be the perfect weekend for you?

2 **WEEKEND**

Do you prefer the weekend over weekdays? Why or why not?

3 **WEEKEND**

Complete the following sentence: My weekend was…

4 **WEEKEND**

What is one thing you wish you did over the weekend, but didn't?

Teambuilding Questions
Kagan Publishing • (800) 933-2667 • www.KaganOnline.com

WEEKEND
Question Cards

5 **WEEKEND**

On a scale of 1 to 10, how would you rate your weekend? Describe your rating.

Teambuilding Questions • © Kagan Publishing

6 **WEEKEND**

Do you have any traditions or activities you do most weekends? Describe.

Teambuilding Questions • © Kagan Publishing

7 **WEEKEND**

What was the funniest thing that happened this weekend? Tell about it.

Teambuilding Questions • © Kagan Publishing

8 **WEEKEND**

Did you see any movies or TV shows this weekend? If yes, describe one in detail. If no, describe one you wish you saw.

Teambuilding Questions • © Kagan Publishing

WEEKEND
Question Cards

---

⑨ WEEKEND

Did you play any sports or games over the weekend? If yes, describe. If no, which sport or game do you wish you played?

Teambuilding Questions • © Kagan Publishing

---

⑩ WEEKEND

Describe one person and how he or she influenced your weekend.

Teambuilding Questions • © Kagan Publishing

---

⑪ WEEKEND

If you could repeat your weekend exactly as it happened, would you? Why or why not?

Teambuilding Questions • © Kagan Publishing

---

⑫ WEEKEND

Did you go anywhere this weekend? If yes, describe where. If no, where do you wish you went and why?

Teambuilding Questions • © Kagan Publishing

WEEKEND
Question Cards

13 WEEKEND

What was the best meal you had this weekend?

Teambuilding Questions • © Kagan Publishing

14 WEEKEND

Weekends are all about fun. Do you agree or disagree?

Teambuilding Questions • © Kagan Publishing

15 WEEKEND

What would be different if the weekend was five days long and the week was only two days?

Teambuilding Questions • © Kagan Publishing

16 WEEKEND

Do you prefer Saturdays or Sundays? Why?

Teambuilding Questions • © Kagan Publishing

WEEKEND
Question Cards

17 | **WEEKEND**

How do you usually feel after the weekend? Explain.

Teambuilding Questions • © Kagan Publishing

18 | **WEEKEND**

Would you rather have a very busy weekend full of activities, or a very slow and relaxing weekend? Explain.

Teambuilding Questions • © Kagan Publishing

19 | **WEEKEND**

What can you do on your weekends that you can never do during the week?

Teambuilding Questions • © Kagan Publishing

20 | **WEEKEND**

How would life be different if there were no weekends? How do you think you could enjoy life without any weekends?

Teambuilding Questions • © Kagan Publishing

Teambuilding Questions
Kagan Publishing • (800) 933-2667 • www.KaganOnline.com

WEEKEND
Journal Writing Question

What would be the perfect weekend for you?

_____

_____

_____

_____

_____

_____

_____

_____

_____

_____

_____

_____

_____

_____

_____

_____

_____

_____

WEEKEND
Journal Writing Question

Do you have any traditions or activities you do most weekends? Describe.

_____

_____

_____

_____

_____

_____

_____

_____

_____

_____

_____

_____

_____

_____

_____

_____

Teambuilding Questions
Kagan Publishing • (800) 933-2667 • www.KaganOnline.com

card set
#20

WHAT WOULD YOU DO IF...

WHAT WOULD YOU DO IF...
Question Cards

WHAT WOULD YOU DO IF...

1

What would you do if you were walking home from school and a suspicious van pulled up right next to you? Has it ever happened to you?

Teambuilding Questions • © Kagan Publishing

WHAT WOULD YOU DO IF...

2

What would you do if you wanted to win the nomination for class president?

Teambuilding Questions • © Kagan Publishing

WHAT WOULD YOU DO IF...

3

What would you do if your parents told you that your family was moving out of state?

Teambuilding Questions • © Kagan Publishing

WHAT WOULD YOU DO IF...

4

What would you do if you saw a student you don't know being bullied? Would you step up? Explain your position.

Teambuilding Questions • © Kagan Publishing

WHAT WOULD YOU DO IF...
Question Cards

WHAT WOULD YOU DO IF...

5

What would you do if you discovered that your best friend said something mean about you behind your back?

Teambuilding Questions • © Kagan Publishing

WHAT WOULD YOU DO IF...

6

What would you do if the cashier gave you back five dollars too much?

Teambuilding Questions • © Kagan Publishing

WHAT WOULD YOU DO IF...

7

What would you do if you had to raise $100 to go on the class field trip?

Teambuilding Questions • © Kagan Publishing

WHAT WOULD YOU DO IF...

8

What would you do if you were hiking through the woods without a cell phone and got lost?

Teambuilding Questions • © Kagan Publishing

WHAT WOULD YOU DO IF...
Question Cards

WHAT WOULD YOU DO IF...

9

What would you do if your parents forgot your birthday?

Teambuilding Questions • © Kagan Publishing

WHAT WOULD YOU DO IF...

10

What would you do if your friends wrote on the bathroom wall and the principal called you in to ask you who did it?

Teambuilding Questions • © Kagan Publishing

WHAT WOULD YOU DO IF...

11

What would you do if you were invited by your crush to go roller-skating, but you have no idea how to roller skate?

Teambuilding Questions • © Kagan Publishing

WHAT WOULD YOU DO IF...

12

What would you do if your brother blamed you for something you did not do?

Teambuilding Questions • © Kagan Publishing

WHAT WOULD YOU DO IF...
Question Cards

---

13 · **WHAT WOULD YOU DO IF...**

What would you do if your friends tried to peer-pressure you into stealing a toy, game, or other item?

Teambuilding Questions • © Kagan Publishing

---

14 · **WHAT WOULD YOU DO IF...**

What would you do if someone wanted to fight with you?

Teambuilding Questions • © Kagan Publishing

---

15 · **WHAT WOULD YOU DO IF...**

What would you do if you received a gift that you didn't really like?

Teambuilding Questions • © Kagan Publishing

---

16 · **WHAT WOULD YOU DO IF...**

What would you do if you were running late for school and you saw a lost, wandering dog on the way?

Teambuilding Questions • © Kagan Publishing

WHAT WOULD YOU DO IF...
Question Cards

WHAT WOULD YOU DO IF...

17 What would you do if you saw one of your classmates cheating on a test?

Teambuilding Questions • © Kagan Publishing

WHAT WOULD YOU DO IF...

18 What would you do if you borrowed something from a friend and then lost it?

Teambuilding Questions • © Kagan Publishing

WHAT WOULD YOU DO IF...

19 What would you do if you were playing handball and everyone was saying that you're out, but you didn't think you were out?

Teambuilding Questions • © Kagan Publishing

WHAT WOULD YOU DO IF...

20 What would you do if you got the opportunity to go to an overseas country to be a foreign exchange student?

Teambuilding Questions • © Kagan Publishing

WHAT WOULD YOU DO IF...
Journal Writing Question

What would you do if you wanted to win the nomination for class president?

_____

_____

_____

_____

_____

_____

_____

_____

_____

_____

_____

_____

_____

_____

_____

_____

_____

WHAT WOULD YOU DO IF...
Journal Writing Question

What would you do if you had to raise $100 to go on the class field trip?

_____

_____

_____

_____

_____

_____

_____

_____

_____

_____

_____

_____

_____

_____

_____

_____

_____

Teambuilding Questions
Kagan Publishing • (800) 933-2667 • www.KaganOnline.com